The International Behavioural and Social Sciences Library

INTERDEPENDENCE AND UNCERTAINTY

TAVISTOCK

The International Behavioural and Social Sciences Library

INDUSTRIAL RELATIONS
In 13 Volumes

INTERDEPENDENCE AND UNCERTAINTY

A Study of the Building Industry

EDITED BY CHARLES CRICHTON

First published in 1966 by
Tavistock Publications Limited

Reprinted in 2001 by
Routledge
2 Park Square, Milton Park, Abingdon, Oxon, OX14 4RN

Transferred to Digital Printing 2007

Routledge is an imprint of the Taylor & Francis Group

© 1966 Building Industry Communications Research Project

The publishers have made every effort to contact authors/copyright holders
of the works reprinted in the *International Behavioural and Social Sciences
Library*. This has not been possible in every case, however, and we would
welcome correspondence from those individuals/companies we have been
unable to trace.

These reprints are taken from original copies of each book. In many cases
the condition of these originals is not perfect. The publisher has gone to
great lengths to ensure the quality of these reprints, but wishes to point
out that certain characteristics of the original copies will, of necessity, be
apparent in reprints thereof.

British Library Cataloguing in Publication Data
A CIP catalogue record for this book
is available from the British Library

Interdependence and Uncertainty
ISBN 0-415-26437-5
Industrial Relations: 13 Volumes
ISBN 0-415-26510-X
The International Behavioural and Social Sciences Library
112 Volumes
ISBN 0-415-25670-4

Interdependence and Uncertainty

A Study of the Building Industry

Digest of a report from The Tavistock Institute

To The Building Industry Communication Research Project

Foreword by Lord James of Rusholme

TAVISTOCK PUBLICATIONS

This book is a condensation of a report prepared for the Building Industry Communications Research Project by the Tavistock Institute, London. The enquiry was undertaken and the original report produced by a social science/operational research team drawn from two units of the Tavistock Institute: Gurth Higgin from the Human Resources Centre, and Neil Jessop, Don Bryant, John Luckman and John Stringer from the Institute for Operational Research.

Condensation and editing of the report for publication was undertaken by Charles Crichton.

First published in 1966
by Tavistock Publications Limited
2 Park Square, Milton Park, Abingdon,
Oxon, OX14 4RN
in 10 point Times Roman, 2 pt leaded
by Burrup, Mathieson & Co., Ltd.
London SE1
© Building Industry Communications
Research Project 1966

Contents

Foreword

The pages which follow describe the first tentative approach to what is really a new and most important project. It is probably true to say that never before has an attempt been made by an industry of the size and scope of the building industry to examine its own procedures, and the relationships between its constituent and widely different interests in this way described here. The inquiry, of which this is a short summary, seems to me to be of genuine importance for at least two reasons. First, the Research Committee, of which I had the honour to be Chairman, was representative of many different interests connected with building which have never cooperated before in any research project of this kind, and this cooperation was itself a fact of great significance. Architects, contractors, quantity surveyors, engineers, building material producers, specialist sub-contractors of various kinds and government agencies were all represented, and all participated in our discussions.

Secondly, the research itself represented an important attempt to bring together two quite different approaches. There was that based on operational research, about which a fair amount is already known. But in addition underlying the work was the realization that many of the problems that arose involved human relationships, so that a sociological study was no less necessary than a logistic one.

No one, least of all the research workers or the sponsors, would claim that the research here described in outline, reached any final conclusions. But it has, at any rate, revealed two vital elements in the situation which we believe must be taken into account in future work. The first is the magnitude of the questions which we are trying to answer. It has become increasingly clear during the two years during which this research has gone on that if the building industry is to reach the degree of efficiency that it should attain, and in view of the country's needs, must attain, not only should there be greater cooperation between its various indispensable elements, but that cooperation must be based on knowledge and not merely on hunches. It is now clear that the acquisition of this knowledge will require research on a considerable scale, continuing over a long period and involving a number of disciplines. It will be research requiring not only the assembly of data but also imaginative thinking and the testing of hypotheses about the structure of a major sector of the economy.

Second, a central question which remains unanswered is how this kind of long-term fundamental research is to be sponsored. The report states unequivocally that the criteria for embarking upon and evaluating such a research must be related in the closest way to the needs of the client, of the users of the building, and of the community. Indeed, one of the most significant facts which emerges from the Report is the central part which the client plays in the efficiency or failure of the building process. It follows, therefore, that the kind of research which is needed must be sponsored not simply by the diverse elements of the building industry itself but by client organizations. Unless they are prepared to collaborate, not simply by a share of sponsorship but by participating in the sometimes uncomfortable experiments and examinations which the research will involve, the changes which are necessary in some of the long-established procedures of the industry will not occur.

The hope of all those concerned with this work, comparatively small scale though it has hitherto been, tentative though its conclusions and exploratory though its methods, is that it may serve as a catalyst to initiate a much larger enterprise of cooperatively sponsored fundamental investigation into what is, after all, one of the most important sectors of our national life.

JAMES OF RUSHOLME

July 1966

Introduction

O, wad some pow'r the giftie gie us
To see ourselves as ithers see us. *Robert Burns*

Had this report been prepared by any individual, or by any group of individuals, working within the building industry using that term in its widest sense, it is probable that some bias would, inevitably, have crept in. There was much to be said, therefore, for entrusting the preparation of the report to professional men not in any way related to the industry, because of the need for an unbiased approach and an objective view of the functions of the industry.

The authors have seen fit at times to use terminology which may be unfamiliar to the reader who works within the building industry. It is appropriate that this should be so because accepted word usages are not always applicable to the thinking underlying the report. It is important that the reader should fully understand the new terminology before embarking on the report itself, therefore a glossary is provided on page xii.

In the work carried out to date a great deal of detailed information was amassed and recorded in a short time as a basis for this report. To have included it all here would have been to carry over into the next stage of research. For this reason and in order to keep the report as concise as possible the thesis on AIDA (Analysis of Interconnected Decision Areas) is only briefly referred to in the precis report on pages 27-33; the matter dealing with the practical application of AIDA has been condensed. Similarly the case studies, which the full report carried in considerable chronological detail, covering a number of different projects, have only been dipped into for factual support of statements in the main text. The extracts are given in Appendix 2 and are linked to the text with reference numbers.

CHARLES CRICHTON

Glossary

Building process
The whole series of activities required between the initiating point of a client's need and the production of a building to fulfil that need.

Client system
The complex of differing interests which today increasingly take the place of an individual client in initiating a building process, e.g. hospital management committee, education committee, etc., etc.

Communications
The network of relationships, technical and social, forming the structure of the building team.

Control functions
The term includes briefing, designing, design quantification, manufacturing, construction control, sub-contracting.

Cost, costs, costing
The words are not used in their accounting sense in this report. They apply to capital expenditure budgeting as well as to cost incurred.

Resource controller
A generic term that may refer to architect, builder, quantity surveyor, engineer, sub-contractor, or supplier, etc.

System of operations
The whole complex of operations, activities and relationships which are initiated by a client's contact with the industry.

Background to the Report

In March 1963 the National Joint Consultative Committee of Architects, Quantity Surveyors and Builders called a conference at Cambridge, representative of the whole building industry. The purpose of the conference was:

(*a*) to receive a Pilot Report on Communications in the Building Industry;[1]

(*b*) to consider further action.

As a result, the conference requested the National Joint Consultative Committee to establish a basis, on an industry-wide scale, for continuing the kind of research represented in the Pilot Report. Thus the Building Industry Communications Research Project was launched.

The next move was envisaged as a 'bridging operation' towards the establishment of a collaborative research institution for the industry.

A Board of Trustees[2] was then set up and a Research Committee was formed and charged with the responsibility of commissioning work and reporting back to the Board of Trustees. This Committee, under an independent chairman,[3] was representative of all sections of the building industry.

The initial research funds were drawn almost equally from the industry and from government sources, and in January 1964 a two-year research project was started.[4]

By February 1965, however, the initial research funds were nearly exhausted and administrative difficulties prevented the launching of an appeal for extra funds. Yet it was essential to prevent the research

1 *Communications in the Building Industry; The report of a Pilot Study*, by Gurth Higgin and Neil Jessop. The Tavistock Institute of Human Relations. This report, issued in a limited edition by the National Joint Consultative Committee of Architects, Quantity Surveyors and Builders, was published in 1965 by Tavistock Publications Limited, price, cloth 25s, paper 12s 6d.

2 See Appendix 4.

3 See Appendix 4.

4 The direct responsibility for the conduct of this project was delegated by the Communications Research Committee to a small steering committee and the project was started by a research team comprising, Gurth Higgin, D. T. Bryant, Neil Jessop, John Luckman, and John Stringer.

coming to a standstill. The steering committee and the research team therefore decided that an interim report should be produced. This decision was influenced by (among other factors) the publication of an official report on *Building Research and Information Services.*[5] Further, there was an atmosphere of uncertainty in the industry which did not encourage an appeal for extra research funds at that time.

The interim report records some of the work carried out by the research team during the first year. It provides an opportunity to reassess the conception and possibilities of the 'bridging operation'.

Reference to the Pilot Report will indicate that the primary source of communications difficulties in the building industry are:

(*a*) the difficulties of definition of the roles of the resource controllers;

(*b*) the complex interaction of the technical, economic, and social forces now operating within, and having effect upon, the industry.

In the sociological field significant changes have taken place during recent years in society's demands on the building industry in relation to:

(*a*) methods of financing building projects;

(*b*) the required size of building projects;

(*c*) the time factor for design and construction.

In the technical field rapid and dramatic development has also taken place, side by side with social change. In the administrative field, however, no comparable metamorphosis has occurred in the roles of those who, jointly and severally, are responsible for controlling the building process. The disparity in development between the social and technical functions on the one hand and the administrative functions on the other is the root cause of difficulties which show up clearly in communications.

This general thesis can best be further explored by providing a 'map' or model of the structure and functions of the industry appropriate to the objectives of the research project.

---

[5] *Building Research and Information Services,* Ministry of Public Building and Works, Spring 1964.

The aim in starting to create such a map has been to put forward hypotheses about the industry's structure and function which may be tested and, if they pass the tests, may lead to practical suggestions for improvements. The agreed research plan anticipated that research in the first year would be mainly concentrated on the operational research aspect, with the sociological study developing in parallel, and a more general study being undertaken to enumerate the non-technical factors that determine the present division of responsibility between all those taking part in the building process.

This report, therefore, starts with an outline of the present situation, based on fieldwork and numerous case studies carried out by the members of the research team. Two important characteristics of the existing pattern which must be incorporated in any map or model of the building process are *interdependence* and *uncertainty*. The origin and features of these characteristics are explored in the first part of the report. The vital sociological aspects of the building process, which must be taken into account as a basis for large-scale research, form the second part. The report concludes with comment and recommendations for future action.

Part 1: Operational research

The present situation

The research project could not encompass the whole building process in detail. But because of the emphasis on communications it was necessary to see the parts played by all members of the building team.

The analytical side of the work was related largely to the open and selective tendering systems, although other contractual systems were studied. Investigations were countrywide and embraced attendance at public seminars, lectures, and conferences; private meetings with architects, surveyors, and builders and others, in addition to conducting a number of detailed case studies.[1] In selecting projects for study we concentrated on those which seemed likely to go well. No purpose was seen in criticizing projects which were obviously inefficient.

Throughout, informants have emphasized that what was observed was normal and that the contracts studied were regarded as 'good' by those concerned. Yet none of the projects studied seemed to live up to expectations. The experience of the team has been of an industry in which misunderstandings, delays, stoppages, and abortive work result from failures in communications, and impressions of confusion, error, and conflict have provided the starting-point for an analysis of the operational characteristics of the building process.[2]

It was found, for example, on one particular case study, that each time a design decision was taken it set in train a chain of consequences which could and did cause the initial decision to be changed, a clear example of how decisions and actions depend on one another (see Appendix 2). Since the full implications of any decision or action can seldom if ever be forecast with absolute accuracy, a communications system which assumes that they can will simply not work.[8]

The first important characteristic to be recognized therefore is interdependence.

[1] A list of the projects studied is given in Appendix 4, page 63.
[2] Actual examples of such failures in communication are referred to in Appendix 2.
[8] Our work in the field of decision-taking led to the development of AIDA (Analysis of Interconnected Decision Areas). The basic principles of this technique are given on pages 27-34.

It was found, too, in all our case studies, that doubts about planning permission, about ownership of land, about approvals and finance bedevilled the briefing and design phases. Uncertainties about the availability of materials and labour upset any attempt to plan an orderly flow of work. Late, faulty, and misinterpreted information also created confusion. Extracts from case studies in Appendix 2 illustrate these findings.

The second important characteristic to be recognized therefore is uncertainty.

Communication channels

These twin aspects of interdependence and uncertainty have been interpreted in terms of communication and information flow. (We are concerned here only with the form of communications channels that exist or should exist, not with the actual content of communications.)

In the existing situation there are two main 'planning activities': the process of design and the organization of contruction.

In the development of each of these activities three principal stages can be identified:

(a) analysis (collection and classification of data);
(b) synthesis (setting up possible solutions or hypotheses);
(c) evaluation (choice of solution).

In construction planning, which is the central operation of the building process, the contractor must take stock of information relating to his own resources and to the resources of others (labour, supplies, equipment, and finance). He must also relate this information to the needs of the building as expressed by the design information he has been given. He must then:

(a) decide what courses are open to him;
(b) make a choice from these;
(c) formulate his choice in terms of a constructive plan.

There are two broadly similar kinds of information flow in the building process. First, at the brief and design stage and, second, at the construction planning stage. In the open tender system the sequence of operation is shown in *Figure 1*.

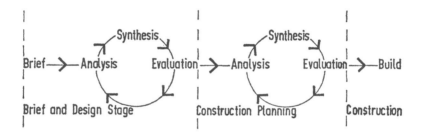

Figure 1   Generalized information flow in the open tender form of the building process

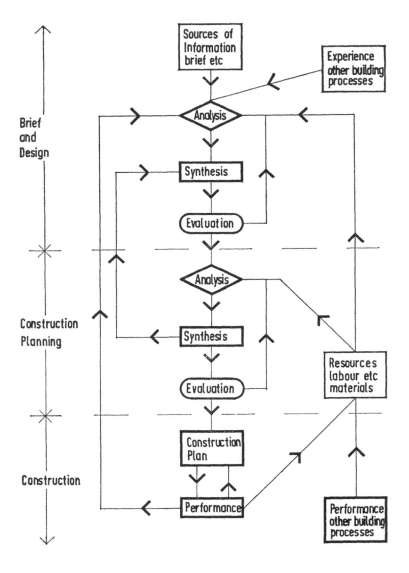

Figure 2. Information flow in an idealized system.

The facing diagram shows information in an idealized system. As in *Figure 1*, the two analysis-synthesis-evaluation circuits are shown linked. The construction phase, however, is divided into two important stages; the plan itself, and the performance measured against the plan in terms of time output, etc. There is naturally full flow of information between these two stages, with the plan being controlled by and partially controlling the performance.

A functional 'box', resources, has been added within the framework of the construction planning and construction phases. Information must flow from here to the analysis stage of construction planning to enable the contractor to formulate his plan. Ideally, information should flow to the analysis stage of brief and design, since any design will depend upon resources for its execution, and information and resources would seem to be one prerequisite for the eventual choice of a suitable design.

The other flows of resource information are the 'feedbacks' to resources from the performance measurements of the construction phases of this and other building processes.

Further 'feedback' loops necessary to an ideally interdependent process are shown on the left.

The contract planning activities may reveal aspects of construction not previously considered. Such information should certainly be taken into account in the design phase by introducing modification to the design if necessary. For this reason, a communication channel between the synthesis stage of construction planning and the synthesis stage of brief and design is shown. This should ensure that designs are formulated that incorporate the necessary requirements of the contractor who is to carry out the work.

The other 'feedback' loop carries information back to the analysis stage of brief and design concerning the performance characteristics of the construction phase. Again this idea is to allow knowledge of eventual circumstances to influence design.

Finally, another input has been added to the analysis stage of the brief and design phase—that of experience from other building processes.

This sequence of operations in the open (and in the selective) tender form of the building process implies that the flow of communication and information is only in one direction. Thus while design affects construction planning, construction planning cannot affect design. The construction planning phase is therefore necessarily constrained to fit the output of the earlier phase. One must inquire, however, whether the information flow of the construction planning sequence might not have had relevance to design; might, in fact, have modified the choices made in design—if the building process had made this possible.

In considering a rational structure for any planning operation (including building) one must suppose that the organization allows for the flow of information that is relevant in a technical sense, from any functional group to any other functional group. One must recognize functional interdependence.

Interdependence

The essence of interdependence in the building process is the relevance of different streams of information to each other in particular contexts. Nothing is more wasteful than the commonly held acceptance of the premise that each task—whether it be briefing or designing, or construction planning or building—should be started afresh from first principles. An ideally interdependent building process is shown, diagrammatically, in *Figure 2* on page 20.

Why doesn't this ideally interdependent system work?

First, the box labelled resources does not fall within a single building process with the result that the links to and from that box can be used to channel only information of a very uncertain nature. Second, the structure of the open tender system, and to a certain extent that of the selective tender system, imposes a division in the building process which blocks the all-important 'feedback' channels of communication. Third, there is no input of commonly shared experience of other building processes: each member of the building team brings little more than his own accumulated experiences—and prejudices—to bear on current problems.

Learning—in the sense of adaptations brought about by experience —is therefore a slow and uncertain process which takes place at an individual level rather than at industry level.

Organizational grouping

When communication flow is broken or blocked, different organizational groupings arise from those that arise when the communication flow is integrated.

In neither case is there a static organization. The organization evolves as the process itself generates needs for different kinds of information. *Figure 3* illustrates the evolving organizational pattern with broken communication flow when the brief and design stage is uncoupled from the construction planning phase.

Figure 3   Evolving organization pattern in the divided case

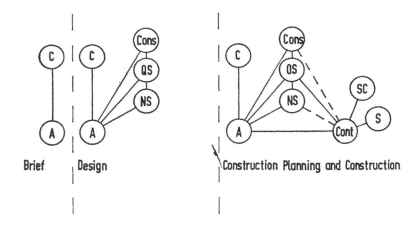

A: Architect C: Client CONS: Consultants QS: Quantity Surveyor NS: Nominated Sub-contractor CONT: Contractor SC: Sub-contractor S: Supplier
The dotted links represent the attempted establishment of communication channels by the contractor with building-team members who were introduced in the design phase.

The evolving pattern when idealized channels of communication are all present is shown in *Figure 4*. In this case, the communication channels between members of the building team emerge at the time demanded by the operations themselves. There is therefore no artificially introduced time-lag in the process since the dovetailing of design and construction planning will clearly shorten the total time of the whole building process.

Figure 4   Evolving organization pattern in the integrated case

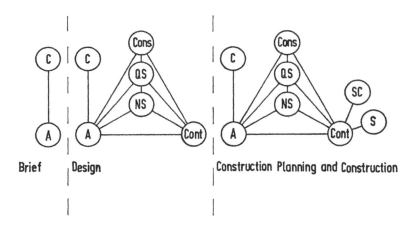

Some of the relationships in this figure are already the subject of further research and the diagram should be interpreted flexibly.

AIDA (Analysis of Interconnected Decision Areas)

The sequential nature of decision-making in the present situation at design stage and, indeed, during the construction stage, has already been commented on on page 22. It is exemplified by one of the case studies (see Appendix 2). While they were engaged on this particular case study, it became clear to the research team that the decisions the design team were attempting to make sequentially were, in fact, affected, not only by what had gone before, but by what was yet to come. The team concluded therefore that consistent decisions could be taken more swiftly and meaningfully if the form of interrelatedness of all the decisions were described at the beginning of the decision-making process. A I D A provides a means of doing this and the following outline procedure explains the general application of the technique.

First, a 'decision area' is defined as an element of the problem where some choice has to be made, for example 'upper-floor materials', 'direction of span of upper floor', 'type of roof'. Second, a 'strategy graph' is produced in which decision areas are shown as points, and relationships between different decision areas are shown as lines joining those points. Third, the strategy graph is expanded into an 'option graph' in the following way.

On examining the decision areas in the strategy graph it is found that each decision area contains a set of choices or 'options'. These options can be defined in such a way that one, and only one, option is selected in the course of making a decision. Links can then be drawn between options in adjacent decision areas that are incompatible. As these option links show incompatibility between the options they join, the number of option links between any two decision areas is a measure of the interdependence between them. Where there are no links the two decision areas are independent of each other.

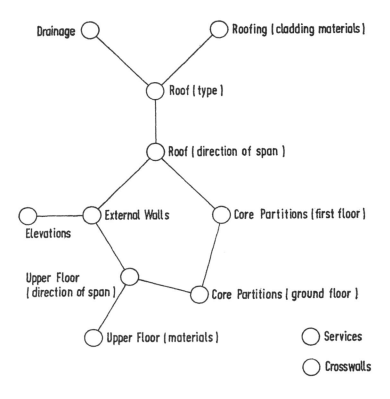

Figure 5 A strategy graph

This strategy graph is related to the case study of the design phase of a house (see Appendix 2). It demonstrates why the sequential taking of decisions created difficulties. Initially, the designers believed that only two of the main decision areas were independent of the remainder, i.e. 'services' and 'crosswalls', allowing a completely free choice in these areas regardless of decisions in other areas. For the remainder, lines drawn between decision areas indicate some degree of interdependence, that is to say, no one choice can be made without reference to one or more of the other choices involved.

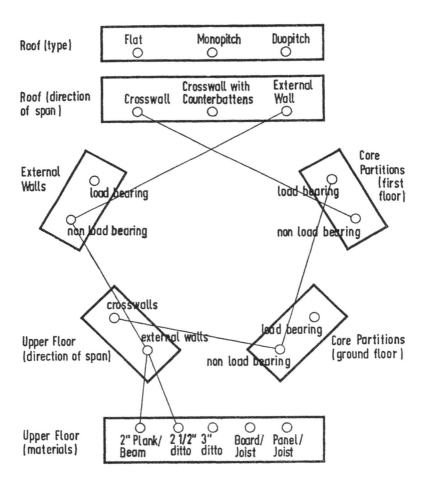

Figure 6 An option graph

This option graph shows that any of the three roof types can be used with any of the three methods of spanning. Reference to the strategy graph shows that when it was being prepared it was thought that a decision on roof types could not be made without reference to roof span: it was not until the nature of the options was examined that the redundancies in the strategy graph were revealed. Similarly, the two decisions (services and crosswalls), believed to be independent on the strategy graph, might be shown to contain incompatible choices when expanded on to the option graph. (It should be remembered that in the option graph, a line joining two options indicates that they are incompatible.)

From this stage onwards it remains to find out all the feasible solutions of the problem and to select the most appropriate solution. For small problems, solutions can be found by simple hand calculations. Large problems might need to be tackled by a computer.

We take up this problem at the stage where a duo-pitch roof has been decided upon. The reduced option graph in *Figure* 7 shows that:

(a) The 'crosswall—counter battens' option in the decision area 'roof—direction of span' has been ruled out on cost grounds.

(b) The option 'board and joist' in the decision area 'upper-floor construction—materials' has been selected, also on cost grounds.

For ease of calculation the decision areas are numbered and the options within the decision areas are lettered.

Figure 7   Reduced option graph

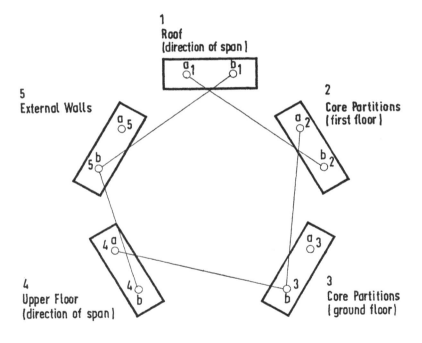

Key: a_1 a_4 : Crosswall a_2 a_3 a_5 : Load-bearing
     b_1 b_4 : External wall b_2 b_3 b_5 : Non-load-bearing

This is a problem which can be solved by simple enumeration of all the possibilities and it can be shown that there are eight feasible solutions, each of which satisfies all the conditions of compatibility. The last part of the problem is to choose one of these eight solutions. To obtain a 'best' solution in this example, the design group were pleased to accept any feasible solution, provided that it cost as little as possible. We costed the options within each decision area. The cheaper option was given a cost of zero, and the more expensive option was given a cost equal to the difference in the cost of the two options. We then compared the total costs of the eight feasible solutions. The solutions and their comparative costs are given in *Table 1* below.

Table 1 Feasible solutions for the circuit of five decision areas

Decision area	Option		Feasible combinations							
			1	2	3	4	5	6	7	8
1. Roof	a_1 Crosswall span	27	1	1			1			
	b_1 External wall span	0			1	1		1	1	1
2. Core partitions	a_2 Load-bearing	6	1	1	1		1	1		
First floor	b_2 Non-load-bearing	0				1			1	1
3. Core partitions	a_3 Load-bearing	11	1	1	1	1	1	1	1	
	b_3 Non-load-bearing	0								1
4. Upper floor	a_4 Crosswall span	0	1	1	1	1				
	b_4 External wall span	13					1	1	1	1
5. External walls	a_5 Load-bearing	23	1		1	1	1	1	1	1
	b_5 Non-load-bearing	0		1						
Total cost of combinations			67	44	40	34	80	53	47	36

The minimum cost solution was, in fact, the same solution that the design group had arrived at independently.

Uncertainty from outside the building process

In addition to the uncertainties arising within the building process as a result of the interdependence of decisions, as discussed above, there is also uncertainty from outside the building process. This uncertainty has two sources. First, there are the uncertainties engendered by the action of those not directly involved in the building process, such as government departments, planning authorities, public bodies, client organizations, and even the general public (see Appendix 2). Second, there are the uncertainties which stem from resources: labour, equipment, and materials. These uncertainties arise mainly because there are a large number of building processes competing for the same resources. Although these uncertainties are outside any one building process, they do arise entirely from within the building industry.

Labour: It is well known that building labour is in short supply and that certain specialist tradesmen, such as plasterers, steelfixers, and bricklayers, are hard to come by in certain areas. Nearly every site we have visited has run into some difficulty with regard to quantity of labour in some form or other. The result of this, despite agreed pay rates, is for the contractor's costs to rise as he strives to maintain his labour force by introducing higher bonuses, extra incentives such as travel allowances, longer hours at overtime rates, and special rates for any work that is the slightest bit different from normal. It is often argued that the contractor should cover himself for such extras in his tender. But any contractor who puts in these expected labour costs is rarely going to win a contract in competition.

High turnover of labour also affects contractors' costs. For any job which is not just unskilled labouring this inevitably means loss of time when new individuals adjust themselves to the task in hand. A study of the turnover of carpenters and labourers on one site showed that both groups had a 'half life' of about four weeks. That is to say, half the men, assumedly starting on the same day, would have left within four weeks.

Most of the steps taken to reduce uncertainty due to labour difficulties stem from the contractor. To ensure adequate labour on site, he uses some or all of the following methods, all involving extra costs:

(*a*) to pay more in wages, bonuses, etc.

(*b*) to employ more sub-contractors with the attendant extra cost of contributing to their profits.

(*c*) to 'encourage' labour to join the permanent staff with pension, sick pay, and holiday benefits.

Methods (*a*) and (*b*) may temporarily solve the problems of the individual contractor. They do nothing for the building industry as a whole. The main benefit arising from method (*c*) is reduction in labour turnover.

Methods which go further towards answering the national problem of labour shortage are:

(*d*) use of more mechanized equipment;

(*e*) use of more manufactured components;

(*f*) designing buildings with forecasted labour availability in mind;

(*g*) more productive use of existing labour.

Mechanization involves finance and maintenance that cannot be met by many smaller contractors.

Equipment and materials: The case-study material, some of which is reproduced in Appendix 2, indicates the kinds of delay and disruption affecting construction programmes caused in connection with the manufacture and supply of materials: too much structural steel, too little cast iron, light fittings too early, windows too late, rusty steelwork, unpainted timber, wrong shapes, holes undrilled, items broken or lost in transit, revisions of prices—all these and many more have been observed during our researches. The time and costs involved in producing volumes of correspondence, making telephone calls, making claims, and so on are enormous.

It is not implied that only suppliers are to blame. Orders placed too late, insufficient attention to detail, wrong schedules, revised drawings, changed construction programmes, and incorrect bills all add to the confusion (see Appendix 2).

The root of the problem is the fact that high demand puts great pressure on the supply system (see Appendix 3).

Uncertainty within the building team

There are four distinct forms which uncertainty within the building team may take—that is to say, uncertainty stemming from the interaction of the various members within any one building team. They are uncertainty of the:
(a) client about members of the design team, and vice versa;
(b) design team members about each other;
(c) client and design team about members of the construction team, and vice versa;
(d) members of the construction team about each other.

Under heading (a), the client is bound to ask such questions as: 'Do I need an architect who specializes in the kind of building I require?' 'Is the architect capable of understanding my requirements?' 'Are the consultants engaged by the architect necessary and, if so, competent?' 'Will I get value for money?'

Similarly, the design team will ask: 'Can the client supply a clear brief?' 'Will he pay promptly?' 'Is there scope for extension of time or money?' 'Will the client's detailed requirements be known early enough?'

Under heading (b), professional men working together may well ask: 'Will I get satisfactory costing information?' 'Will the architect's drawings be ready for coordination with mine?' 'Will the flow of design information be satisfactory?' 'Will drawings be complete by the time the Bill of Quantities is required?' 'Will the architect's form of design be capable of interpretation without ambiguity?'

Under heading (c), uncertainty must arise in an industry that is formally organized so that design and construction are treated as two separate and isolated phases. Inevitably, client and design team will ask: 'Will main and sub-contractors be able to execute the design satisfactorily?' 'Will they be able to cope with special features or equipment?' 'Will they act like reasonable men when it comes to changes in design and resulting variation orders?'

Contractor and sub-contractor will ask: 'Has the building been designed with the builder in mind?' 'Is there and will there be sufficient detail for a satisfactory job?' 'Will design information be ready for efficient construction planning?' 'Will the client pay promptly?'

Under heading (d), typical questions are: 'Is this sub-contractor's work up to my standard?' 'Will the contractors allow me to progress my work satisfactorily?' 'Does the contractor use adequate planning and management methods to achieve coordination of work?'

Attempts to lessen these uncertainties are made in various ways. For example, the nomination of sub-contractors, selective tendering, negotiated contracts, and the package deal tend to reduce the uncertainties between the client/design team group and the construction team. The package deal or all-in service, for instance, allows the builder to contribute to decisions on design, thereby reducing uncertainty in this field.

Existing management tools, such as work study and critical-path planning, can, if properly and consistently used, play a big part and could play an even larger part in reducing uncertainties and improving communications. Unfortunately, too many organizations have relegated these and other ideas to the backroom instead of applying them as a central part of the organizational machinery of construction planning and control.

Criteria for improvement

In speaking of better communications we are speaking of forms of organization which will enable information essential to the creation of a building to be channelled where and when it is needed. We are also concerned to see that the skills of the people involved are not wastefully used. Different form of organization have to be considered in relation to the varying powers to intervene in the building process possessed by members of the building team and by others. If the form of organization is changed, then the power of intervention of each member of the building team is likely to become different from what it is now.

We have only to consider the diversity of interests involved among architects, quantity surveyors, engineers, builders, sub-contractors, suppliers, and labour, on the one hand, and clients with varying requirements, local authorities, building users, planners, the public, and the government, on the other hand, to realize that there is not likely to be a single generally accepted criterion for improvement. Such a criterion would have to take account of the costs and incentives of all the parties, as well as of matters of time, security, amenity, functional success, environmental contribution, rateable value, prestige, and so on.

Thus it can be seen that, over and above the operational problems that call for long-term research on an industry-wide basis, there are problems whose impact on the building industry has not hitherto been sufficiently appreciated. These problems must be explored side by side with operational research. The next section of the report provides a starting-point for such research by examining the competitive tender system through a socio-technical analysis.

Part 2: Sociological research

This section on sociological research, having been undertaken in parallel with the operational research, will show themes and approaches common to the foregoing section of the report.

The client

Since the building process is initiated by a client, we preface our remarks in this section with the relationship between the client and the building industry.

The generally held view of relationship between the professional activator of the building process within the industry and the lay initiator of the process outside the industry is that of the architect 'taking a brief from his client'. This concept, which is essentially that of one individual communicating his requirements to another individual, is implicit within the traditional thinking of the building team. The concept, for most building projects of any size today, is obsolescent, if not obsolete, as a true representation of the relationship between the building industry and the society it serves. In the overwhelming majority of cases, the client is not an individual. 'The client' is a complex system of differing interests and 'the client's' relationship is seldom with a single member of the building industry. Even if initiated through individuals, the relationship rapidly becomes a conference between groups of both sides.

The client system may be an industrial or commercial organization, a hospital management committee, an education committee, or one of many other forms of organizational system. These client systems, as within the system of the building industry, are made up of both congruent and competing sets of understandings, values and objectives. Much design and even building work has proved to be abortive because unresolved or unrecognized conflicts of interests or objectives within the client system have only come to light after the building process has been initiated (see Appendix 2). If the building industry is to provide optimum solutions to the building needs of such clients, this pattern of forces must be fully taken account of.

If the industry is to provide the best possible service to society, we would suggest that all in the industry who are involved in the initial relationships with client systems need to be very much more aware and responsible in developing the brief through a more conscious understanding of the whole field of social forces they must work with.

The research team formed the clear impression that in its relationships with its client systems the building industry, not only does not take sufficient account of the complexity of organizations it is dealing with, but also tends to be impatient of this complexity. It is suggested that the members of the building team, in addition to acquiring greater awareness of social forces, should better equip themselves for joint action with the client system by developing logical techniques for clarifying and resolving the problems of interdependent decisions.

Of equal importance with the development of the necessary skills for problem analysis and synthesis and understanding of social contexts, is the need to set up an appropriate structure of relationships to ensure their effective use. On the one hand, such a structure must allow for the inevitable separate contributions to the common scheme from different specialities, including those from the client system. On the other hand, it must avoid the different contributions developing too far without cross-reference to others whom their decisions implicate, and of any of the potential interveners being left behind the growing scheme, to intervene later with demands for reconsideration. Even with such a carefully designed structure, there will be difficulties; but, without it, confusion, delays, and abortive work are inevitable.

To avoid these difficulties, there needs to be a very early acceptance among all concerned of binding procedures for a strict phasing of decision stages—with intercommunication—and of agreed rules for returning to report to all the potential interveners relevant to the different stages of the developing scheme.

A socio/technical analysis based on competitive tendering procedure

The true starting-point for this phase of our research is the position arrived at in the Pilot Study, with particular reference to the competitive tender system. This has been taken as a starting-point, not only because it is the most common form of contract relationship in the industry, but also because it is the basic form from which all others can be seen to have developed.

The primary unit of study has been the building process. In this system is not included the client, who, as explained earlier, belongs within a system of his own, external to the industry, having functions and interests quite separate from the industry, yet closely implicated with the building process and with a high degree of interpenetration between the two systems.

We have endeavoured to produce, or at least start on, a 'map' of the industry and, as this map develops, it becomes clear that within the building process there are five closely locked sub-systems. These are:

(*a*) a system of operations;
(*b*) a system of resource controllers;
(*c*) a system of formal controls (directive functions);
(*d*) a system of informal controls (adaptive functions);
(*e*) a system of social and personal relations.

A system of operations

To move from the initiating point of a client's need through to the production of a structure, a whole series of operations must be undertaken. These can be described as a system of operations without reference to the way in which responsibility for them and their control is undertaken.

At the start of the building process many resources of information, skill, materials, and equipment need to be brought together in response to the requirements of the system of operations. Information must be gathered from the client about his needs: general decisions must be made in detail to achieve the general conception through all the processes of construction; anticipation of costs and control of expenditure must be made at many points: the physical operations and acquisition of materials must be taken into account.

Our analysis of this sub-system attempts to understand the intrinsic nature of the relationships between these various operations—free of assumptions about human control functions.

The chain of operations so conceived can, of course, take many forms. Our object is to understand the characteristics of this total chain against the criteria of the simplest, the most rational and the least redundant way of setting them up in terms of both events and time.

Questions of cost and criteria concerning the adequacy of function for the purpose of the structure and of the nature of the contribution it will make to the built environment are not relevant at this stage of the analysis because they belong to the area of interaction between the client, on the one hand, and economic and social values, on the other, and these cannot be determined apart from their application in any one case. The optimum conditions for the chain of operations thus conceived will obviously be an ideal. It has value, however, in helping to provide an answer to the question: 'Does this form of organization allow the basic operations of the building process to be realized more effectively than any other?'

More complete research is necessary to be fully clear about the nature of all the operations in building and the optimum conditions for their functioning. Work to date has indicated that there are certain inherent qualities in the system of operations that any control system must take account of if it is to achieve any degree of effective control. No part of the process can, in practice, be isolated from the whole and worked on in any meaningful way without a constant need for cross-reference to other parts—interdependence.

In Part 1, the twin characteristics of interdependence and uncertainty have been discussed. In conditions of interdependence and uncertainty the phasing of decision-taking can be crucial. If, in the face of uncertainty, decisions are delayed until fuller information is available, dependent operations can be badly held up. If, on the other hand, apparently safe decisions are taken too early and too finally, they may create intolerable constraint on later developments. Constant and comprehensive attention needs to be given to the phasing of decision throughout the process.

Given any degree of specialization in responsibility for control functions in building, confusion, delay, and unnecessary work will result if the inherent factors of uncertainty and interconnectedness are not recognized. In undertaking briefing, design, costing or construction planning, for example, there are limits, probably coming much sooner than is usually recognized, beyond which it is fruitless to proceed until some feedback from moves already taken is available. It is necessary to check the validity of steps already taken, as well as to indicate the possibilities and direction of the next steps. To assign such a function to one part of the process, to demand finality and feasible completion of it within a given phase, is unrealistic.

A system of resource controllers

We turn now to the human activities applied to control functions: these we ignored in the previous section. There are a series of roles which control the application of the many varied resources (including knowledge and skills) that are required to develop and maintain the system of operations. These roles, which are defined in terms of particular aspects of the operations and the type of resource they contribute, together constitute a system of resource controllers. None of these roles is a contemporary development. All take their basic definition from conditions in the industry at the time they were developed. In each case, the role was developed as an answer to social, economic, and technical problems present at the time. Since their inception, the functions of these roles have become more specifically defined in terms of the resource and control for which they take responsibility. Further, the roles, as so defined, have become entrenched and protected within institutes, federations, and associations designed to protect the interests of those carrying them. The conditions that gave rise to these roles have changed over time, but their definitions have changed little, if at all. Indeed, the characteristic reaction of their protective institutions has been one of more rigid defence of the roles as traditionally defined. In general, institutional preoccupations have become increasingly inward-looking and defensive in the face of external changes.

The first reaction of any of the institutions and associations to a new development in the organization of the building team tends to be concerned with the implications for its members of the change, rather than with the effect on the effectiveness of the total building process. The overall result is a tendency to freeze all resource controller roles within definitions that are increasingly inappropriate to the changing social, economic, and technical conditions under which the building process must proceed in the contemporary world.

Although most members of the building team recognize that they cannot undertake even their own given responsibility without the wider considerations that it calls for, none is willing to allow serious intrusions into his area by another. In this way, although all recognize the difficulties involved, all, when wearing their formal hats, are nevertheless held within inappropriately exclusive limits of function and responsibility. Fortunately, people can, and do, cheat in carrying out formal roles, so collaboration of a more practical kind is possible . . . informally.

A system of formal controls (directive functions)

There exists a formal system by means of which all the traditionally-defined resource controllers control and take responsibility for the operations of the building process. This system is characterized by the same sort of mutual exclusiveness that one finds in the roles of those involved in it.

The formal system comprises a series of theoretically exclusive operations applied in sequence to the different phases of the building process. The system is formal in that theoretically it is the way in which the control of the building process works. It is commonly understood. It can be explained. It forms the basis of written information about the building process.

The first characteristic of the formal system is the independence of the control functions. Briefing, designing, design quantification, construction planning and control, manufacturing, sub-contracting, and so on, are all set out as functions which can be controlled by a role independent of, and institutionally protected from, others. The system is also characterized by a non-continuous or sequential application of the control functions. It is assumed that, at some point, lines can be drawn marking the beginning and completion of any activity whose position in control of the building process is then taken over by another. The system has a characteristic of *sequential finality*.

This formal system of controls, or directive functions, is not very directly manifested in actual behaviour and, if our information were based only on the behaviour of the building team on the job, we might never have become aware of the formal system in its true form. It is easily understood, however, from what people say when describing their jobs as distinct from what they do. It is even more readily understood from writings about the building process.[4]

A social system—in this case a group of people systematically sharing control of a common process—in which relationships are based on mutual independence, and where contributions to the common task are based on sequential finality, does not seem suited effectively to control a process characterized by the interdependence of its operations, fraught with uncertainty and requiring carefully phased decisions and continuous application of all control functions.

The research suggests that the discrepancy between the demands of the system and actual behaviour arises because the characteristics

---

[4] *A Code of Procedure for Selective Tendering*, National Joint Consultative Committee of Architects, Quantity Surveyors & Builders (London 1959).
The Architect's Guide to Running a Job, Ronald Green, Architectural Press (London 1962).
Building Project Management: A Guide to Procedure, National Joint Consultative Committee of Architects, Quantity Surveyors & Builders (London 1963).
Handbook of Architectural Practice and Management, Royal Institute of British Architects (London 1963/65).

of the formal system are so much in conflict with the control functions required to achieve effectiveness in the system of operations
that, in practice, the formal system cannot be closely followed.
Rigid adherence to the procedures of the formal system would not
be possible, under normal conditions, without unacceptable expenditure—particularly of time. In practice, reality forces a recognition
of interdependence, uncertainty, phased decision-taking, and the
continuous application of functions. It forces members of the building team to adapt themselves.

A system of informal controls (adaptive functions)

Although the forms of behaviour discussed in this section are considered not to be the normal procedures, they are, in fact, much more
normal than the procedures of the formal system. These forms of
control are drawn from direct observation of the building team at
work and from talks with them about what they were doing. Most
of their forms of behaviour are undertaken quite consciously and
their existence is known to all members of the building team. They
are, nevertheless, informal in that they are not spoken of on the
record; nor would they appear in the handbooks or formal reports
and literature of the industry—except as procedures to be avoided.

Despite this, the informal procedures seem to give greater recognition to the inherent interdependence between the operations of the
building process than is found in the sequential finality demanded
by the formal system. The informal procedures seem to produce
more realistic phasing of decisions, more continuous application of
control functions, and more realistic flexibility in face of the inevitable uncertainties that all must accept.

The building industry is not unique in having formal and informal
sets of behaviours for tackling its problems. What is important in
the present case is, first, the extent to which the building process
depends on the application of the informal system to function
adequately; second, the disparity between the characteristics of the

formal and informal systems in relation to the needs of the real task with which they are concerned.

The R I B A's recently published handbook lays down that, after a scheme design has been arrived at and before the detailed design is undertaken, 'the brief should not be modified after this point'. In real life such a demand of the formal system can seldom, if ever, apply. It makes the assumption that the client's system ceases changing or developing in any way at that point. The developing processes of detailed design and of construction generate information which challenges, if not compels, changes in original conceptions which have a direct effect on function, cost or some other aspect of the brief.

It is reasonable to assume that, as the scheme develops, and more information about what he is going to do becomes available to the client, he will be very likely to modify his decision in many ways. Similarly, is it reasonable to expect designers to produce the 'best' answers to a problem in terms of cost, function, and good architecture before the implications for detailed design and even construction of their initial decisions become clear?

In fact, clients and designers seldom accept these constraints, and changes in the brief therefore continue to be fed into the process at all times. Indeed, the formal system allows for this through the variation order. The same is true of the design phase. In formal theory, design is complete at an early stage. Not only is information expected to be complete at this time, but it is also considered to be feasible in terms of 'buildability' and cost.

In practice, this is not possible, and even the formal system recognizes this by provisional items in the Bill of Quantities. But there are many other aspects of the design—not covered by provisional items—that are incomplete. This particularly applies to the design of services: the reason for this is related to the sequential manner in which the design process is usually handled.

The hierarchy customarily followed is from architect to structural engineer, and then to the services—usually in the order: heating and ventilation, electrical, plumbing, and gas—not to mention telephones, internal and external. Often those services towards the end of the chain are asked only for a very general layout at the design stage.

In practice, many details of services design are worked out on the job, during tours of the work after site meetings, for example. This tendency is encouraged by a certain withdrawn protectiveness on the part of those responsible for 'service' design, who express distrust of the architect's ability to build their work satisfactorily into the design and of the quantity surveyor's ability to measure it accurately.

In theory, the quantity surveyor preparing for full competitive tender should quantify the design in full detail. In practice, of course, he seldom, if ever, has sufficient information. He has to extemporize and include what he expects architect and client may want.

Now the formal system requires that, before Bills of Quantities are prepared, full working drawings shall be completed. According to the R I B A handbook, these drawings will embody: 'Final decision on every matter related to design, specification, construction and cost, and full design of every part and component of the building'. Then, in heavy type, comes the warning 'any future change in location, size, shape or cost after this time will result in abortive work'.

These precepts assume that those responsible for the building process at this point are independent, autonomously self-controlling, and that they can produce enough information from within their own system for reliable decision. This is patently not the case. In fact, they cannot arrive at reliable decisions about cost, construction, specification or design without interaction with all those with whom they must share responsibility for control and completion of the building process. Informal practice, recognizing this reality, follows procedures the reverse of the formal theory.

The contract, in theory, is arrived at as a result of tendering procedure which is considered to be a legally and commercially rational bargain between the client and the builder—generally the builder who can undertake the work most cheaply. This view is based on the assumption that all details of the project have been finally decided and are specified in detail in the tender documents, and that the contractor can anticipate accurately at this time what all his costs will be. This is not so and it is not surprising, therefore, that the builder's pricing and the client's acceptance of any competitive tender must always be acts of faith.

As an insurance against uncertainty, some builders' estimators take protective action of various kinds. Knowing that this goes on, some quantity surveyors anticipate these actions and arrange items in the bills to offset the estimators' actions.

Sometimes, if a builder prices on the basis of particular knowledge of a site, he may lose the job. He will, therefore, suppress his information and hope, when it comes to light, to cover the extra cost. If he succeeds, then the client finds that his final expenditure is above what he contracted for.

At, or about, the time of contract, a programme is required of the builder. This programme will be produced and agreed. But such agreement cannot be undertaken at this stage except by a collusion in acceptance of unreality by all parties. It is not possible to put exact dates to specified phases of the project at this time. The future holds too much uncertainty. Such a programme can only be based on assumptions about the variety, quantity and timing of future application of resources. Everybody knows this. But, hopefully, detailed programmes are frequently set up and agreed by all—formally. Informally, protective action is taken by the client, and/or his advisers, keeping a period in hand; by the builder relying on some delay for which he can disclaim responsibility and claim an extension of time.

This persistence in unreal assumptions has led to the often uncritical and inappropriate application of techniques of 'scientific management'. We have yet to see such techniques used as true planning tools. Usually, they are abandoned in the face of the inevitable uncertainties encountered. At best, they are kept up to date after the event as a record.

In spite of this, however, we have been impressed on occasions by the fact that the abandonment has not caused jobs to lag as much as the techniques suggest they should. The reason, of course, is that informal (and, within one definition, unscientific) management practices, calling for almost hour to hour redeployment by an experienced site manager, have kept the job going without undue delay or the generation of unacceptable cost.

This informal management has disadvantages—it reduces the programming time scale to a week or a day, so that long-term programming is often overlooked. It produces a climate of endemic crisis which becomes self-perpetuating. The type of man who can best handle this situation tends to have a crisis type of personality. He thrives on this situation and is unwilling to entertain the possibility or validity of any form of planning and control that is not short-term and completely flexible. The inappropriate use of mechanistic management tools, such as the critical path method, reinforces the approach of such men and leads to antagonism to all control techniques.

A system of social and personal relations

The attempt to operate an inappropriate formal control system, coupled with an adaptive but non-responsible informal system, inevitably produces personal and group stresses and problems for all concerned. As might be expected, it is in the later stages of the project (when the ineffectiveness of the process control procedures are nearing their confrontation with the realities of time, cost, and quality of product) that these stresses begin to be felt.

Up to the time of the contract, those responsible for briefing, cost estimating, and designing, will have taken account informally of the realities of uncertainties to come. But in their formal behaviour in setting up and taking the client's interests into the contract—the move that takes the contract beyond their exclusive control—they, and the builder with them, will agree a bargain as if the future held no uncertainty. It is assumed that delayed decisions from the contract phase, uncompleted details and formalities, costing of provisional sums, will not raise problems nor cause delay. It is assumed, too, that all physical conditions on which progress will depend will be easily coped with and that resources will be sufficiently under control by those responsible for them not to interfere with the conditions. Thus are agreements made by men wearing formal hats. But, off the record, all parties will have reservations. Uncertainty is recognized, but faith is placed upon its advantageous outcome.

Conditions about time are usually the earliest to create problems. Almost all tender invitations call for acceptance by the builder of a given time for completion, or for the builder's statement on this. No builder tendering in competition, and hoping to be successful, dares to reject a completion date asked for, or to put in other than a hopefully low estimate of the time required. Because each knows that, by doing so, he may lose the work.

Having had such a time condition accepted contractually, the design team sighs with relief at having passed the responsibility to the builder. The builder, in his turn, doubtful about the realization of the programme, is alert from this point on, through all stages of the project, to point out the various sources of delay which are outside his control. But, having had the time and cost conditions accepted in the contract, the design team, usually through the architect, will inform the client that he will get his building at a given time for a given cost.

As delays and extra costs inevitably arise throughout the process, so the social control mechanisms set up to manage the work become less and less capable of undertaking this function. As a result, all concerned become increasingly involved in acrimonious attempts to place, or, more usually, to avoid, responsibility for these discrepancies.

What has been said of the unreality underlying the relationships between builder and design team is equally true of his relationship with (among others) sub-contractors and suppliers who are particularly sensitive to interference from uncertainty, and so are very active in anticipating defences for the programme responsibilities they have undertaken. Any hint from the builder, or his staff, that the job will not be ready for the sub-contractor, as formally programmed, will be noted to be produced later as justification for delay. In the meantime, with delay on all his jobs, the sub-contractor will concentrate resources where they are most profitably to be used for him, and greater delay on the original job will result.

At the inevitable progress meeting, the needs of the job will be lost in attempting to settle responsibility for broken agreements irresponsibly undertaken by all parties. At such formal meetings—in theory set up to meet the management needs of the project—all are imprisoned by their collusive acceptance of unreal, independent accountability for parts of an interdependent responsibility.

Although the reasons for these situations are commonly seen in personal terms—incompetence, laziness, or financial greed of others for example, and although bitterness, and even hurt, can be given by accusations in such terms—these behaviours are seldom crucial. An observer can see that such behaviour is forced on those concerned by the demands of their roles in the system, rather than by personal motivation. Dissatisfaction is the most usual residue of such experiences. Few can leave such meetings without a distasteful feeling of self-inflicted offence to their self-respect as professionals, tradesmen or craftsmen.

Because of their responsibility to others, professional men are particularly sensitive to such personal reactions. The architect, for example, who—perhaps for good reasons—has departed from formal procedures in delaying a decision or decisions, has also been party to the original agreement about time and cost. Moreover, he has allowed these to become expectations of his client. Because of his own departures from the 'proper' procedures, he cannot free himself from involvement in the rather confused responsibility for not realizing their targets. He is then in a very difficult position in reporting the situation to the client, because he cannot be entirely frank without risking the charge of incompetence.

Cost handling

Finally, a word must be said about the effects of the division of functions on the handling of costs. There are three principal ways in which costs are handled at different stages of the building process. (a) During design. Cost information is provided in the form of a cost plan which is based on an estimate of the cost contribution of each of the main elements in the design.

(b) At the contract. Costs are handled through a highly particularized breakdown in the bill, based on trade divisions.

(c) At account. Costs are handled by a mixture of certificates (based on work done over a given time—this may cover many trades and many elements in the building), of variations (which can be based on bill rates or special agreed rates) and daywork and other extras (based on the builder's private system of costing).

These three systems of money handling cannot, without making many assumptions, be related one to another nor validated one against another. As long as responsibility for the different parts of the process and its costs are so divided with independence and even mistrust between the parties, it would seem impossible to get a more rational system for costing the whole.

A comparative discussion of other contractual arrangements

At the present time there are two main types of attack on the problem of the unsatisfactory nature of the organization, functioning and communications in the building industry: First, exhortations to return to the formal system in its pure form. Second, a call for some new formal system which incorporates the more adaptive characteristics of the informal system.

Those in favour of reinstating the formal system argue that it would be adequate if adhered to rigidly by all parties. In this view the informal system is deplored. Its procedures are regarded as aberrations from the normal, occasioned by laxity or cupidity of various parties trying to cut corners or secure financial advantage for themselves. If it did not exist, all concerned would pay more attention to following formal procedures and all would be well.

From our analysis, it would appear that this approach is misguided and is bound to fail. On our thesis, the informal system only exists because the formal system intrinsically has characteristics which are incapable of handling effectively the system of operations required for the building process. The informal system is not the lazy man's way out but a means of adaptation that is essential for the formal system to work at all.

The objection to some new system is that, once the basic responsibility relations of the existing formal system are disturbed, the client, as the general paymaster, is going to suffer. The present competitive system is said, by its supporters, to be the only one which will, in an open market, give the client any guarantee that he can make a bargain in terms of time and cost and that will give him contractual protection. The validity of this statement seems doubtful. How many clients, faced with discrepancies of time and cost at the end of a project feel satisfied that the competitive market has given them protection? [5]

Many professionals say that the penalty clause in contracts can seldom, if ever, be invoked effectively and they advise clients against competitive tender as being unable, in a situation of uncertainty about all the factors affecting time and cost, to provide the basis for a valid and protective contract. Builders are alleged to indulge in sharp practice unless there are pre-agreed contractual limits. But builders accuse clients and advisers of sharp practice when they indulge in cheeseparing and legalistic quibbles. In fact, the behaviour of all parties in the situation is inevitably determined by the nature of the system in which they are involved. It generates self-protection and suspicion. The increasing number of building organizations with sophisticated management and growing reputations for commercial integrity suggests that a different pattern of relationships for all concerned might reduce the self-protection and suspicion.

Attempts to achieve a wider coordination of control of the building process have been made in recent years and they fall under five main headings:

(a) the professional consortium;

---

[5] The Director of Building Management, DGRD, at the Ministry of Public Building & Works was quoted in 'Scientific Business' February 1965, as follows: 'Tenders exceeding estimates by large margins are still a disaster faced by clients . . . so long as tendering is a common means of establishing the cost of building, there will always be an element of surprise in what the client finally has to pay.'

(b) the construction consortium;
(c) the package deal;
(d) the client consortium;
(e) the professional coordinator.

The professional and construction consortia are both attempts to coordinate the activities of resource controllers within one area of similar values and economic relationships. Neither form is sufficiently well-established to have disclosed clearly the nature of any change they may bring about. Both are claimed to allow a more effective pattern of control and communications than in the more rigidly divided formal pattern. Neither tackles the most difficult problem in coordination—namely, the interface between the professional and the commercial areas of the industry. Both should go far towards overcoming the difficulties that arise from serial contribution of:

(a) different designs, and
(b) those responsible for different parts of the construction process.

The least tried means of providing greater coordination in the industry is that of professional coordinator, who acts as sponsor for the whole building process, having the only direct contact with the client. The case for such an all-powerful role can be strongly made; but within the present structure it produces universal suspicion and a sense of threat. To be acceptable, the development of such a function would require a joint redefinition of all roles in the building team in relation to the new function, in terms that would reduce the sense of threat. Although it has appeared in America and has been offered in this country, the role of professional coordinator is currently little more than a concept.

The package deal attempts to provide overall co-ordination by the builder. Interdependence and phased decision-taking are claimed in its favour. Through concurrent, rather than serialised control functions, it is said to produce buildings quicker and at lower cost than the formal procedure. The counter-claim is that, with a commercial controlling interest, bad quality inevitably results. Domination by the builder is regarded as a serious threat by the professions.

Similar claims and counter-claims are made for the client consortia. But here there is a complementary difficulty in that those concerned with the construction phase, but excluded from the consortia, feel threatened by the vast concentrations of client and professional power: threats to commercial freedom of movement and the fear that growth of such consortia would effectively dominate, if not eliminate, the entrepreneurial market. Nevertheless, both the package deal and the consortia encourage system building, a trend which must be given consideration.

The negotiated contract has the claimed advantage that the builder, by being brought in earlier, can contribute to design decisions. In our own experience, this advantage can only be partially exploited, for may not the builder adopt defensive practices, for example, by using his influence to affect design to his own advantage when tendering, rather than for the benefit of the project as a whole? Our own experience and published sources give little information about the cost, time and quality effects of the negotiated contract.

Part 3: Indications for future research

There are many different objectives to which improvement in communications could refer. An improvement, seen from one viewpoint, may be undesirable change when seen from another. Research, therefore, must be directed positively towards realistic proposals for effecting change. As we have said, there is not likely to be a single, generally-accepted, criterion for improvement. Such a criterion would have to take account of the costs and incentives of all the parties, as well as matters of time, security, amenity, prestige, and so on.

Apart from the diverse 'values' which prevail among members of the building team, they have become conditioned to working in an atmosphere of uncertainty. Uncertainties are either basically organizational or due to outside factors, such as government policy, economic and social climate, labour, materials, weather, and so on. This atmosphere is all-pervasive and has greatly contributed to the habits of mind of participants with respect to each other. It is responsible for the style of management in the industry. Because of uncertainty, the pinning-down of responsibility becomes a matter of player's skill. Existing management tools could play a far larger part in reducing uncertainty but too often they are ignored. Habits are difficult to alter, even when the cause is understood and action taken to effect a cure. Crisis management is likely to persist. To a degree, the industry has a tacit loyalty to present conditions for reasons of immediate partisan advantage.

Nothing contributes more to the industry's inefficiencies than uncertainty, since it provides the ideal environment for conflict. It can be asserted that there is a widespread wish to see changes brought about, that is to see a new stage in the industry's long evolution. Natural evolution may seem to be the proper vehicle for change. But natural evolution is a process of waste, makeshift, compromise, and blunder.[6] The goal for future research should be to seek the benefits of natural evolution, but with a dispatch which the natural process lacks.[7] What then is the role of future research?

[6] P. Medawar—Reith Lectures 1959.
[7] One example of the natural evolutionary process at work has been the recent proliferation of building 'systems' when it was always clear that only a handful could survive to economic viability.

First, there must exist genuine possibilities for new forms of organization in techniques of communication. Research must be aimed at discovering more about forms of organization and contractual arrangements, other than those touched on in this report. A fully comprehensive analysis and critical evaluation of all such developments would provide the necessary data for specifying the characteristics of future forms of organization that are desirable and feasible. The most desirable form of organization would permit a much wider co-ordination of control to be achieved, so as to reduce the uncertainties which result from the present artificial division between design and construction planning cutting across the information feedback link which is so vital to the effective functioning of the building process.

Research can be aimed at suggesting new forms to try. In preparing this report, we have already carried out work on one suggestion. This we have called A I D A—'Analysis of Interconnected Decision Areas' (see pages . . . .). This mathematical system involves the structuring of a problem into decision areas; the description of the decision area in terms of a graph; the expansion of the strategy graph into an option graph; and, finally, the determination of the feasible solutions to the problem. The concepts of A I D A have been developed in order to suggest approaches to some of the more fundamental problems with which this research was to have been concerned. These deal with the possibilities for redefining roles and relationships. The starting-point is that decisions have to be taken: they may have to be taken by more than one person: and decisions cannot be taken in isolation. Much of the work on A I D A is speculative but it might, therefore, form a basis for further research in the sphere of redefining roles and relationships in the building industry with the object of effecting changes.

Research, then, must be aimed at measuring the effects which changes have or would have. These measurements must be sufficiently sensitive to distinguish between proposals, and this means setting up, either as theoretical models or as real life experiments, conditions which simulate the changes under study.

Finally, it must be possible to say, in relation to the effects of any proposed change, whether it will represent an improvement on what has gone before. In other words, research of an operational kind can only proceed if it is undertaken from a definite standpoint representing the goals of those who wish to pursue improvement. It cannot remain at a purely descriptive and impartial level.

The only set of objectives, in our view, which has any chance of wide acceptance, is the set belonging to the client/user/community complex. We must consider what the client wants, what the user needs, and what the community and its representatives consider important. There is good reason to believe that making communications in building serve the customer is wholly consistent with the well-being of the industry itself.

A logical analysis should be made of the various kinds of building/ client system and of the relative advantages to be expected for the participants under a supposed set of fee/contract arrangements. The possibility that unreal conflict situations may be exposed for what they are, leading to a lessening of resistance to change, provides a strong motive for carrying out this kind of research. Such analysis is, we believe, an essential prerequisite to the introduction of new organizational forms in the industry.

After measuring the effects of change, the next task must be that of measuring the efficiency of any building process from the point of view of the client/user/community.

The difficulty of obtaining suitable scales of measurement is illustrated by the problem of evaluating the consequential effects of a delay. A job takes longer than was planned—but how realistic was the plan? The next job starts late—but what scope has been provided for replanning to minimise the effect? If replanning had been done—would shortage of material have been revealed when it would otherwise have gone undetected? Certainly, the effect which improved communications would have cannot be measured by piecemeal calculation from individual incidents. The field of measurement must be the complete building, rather than an individual feature of its design or construction.

If we are to say that one form of building process is better than another—and by how much—we must develop some scale on which to base such statements. There is probably no single characteristic, such as time, cost, function, amenity, which will be appropriate to measure the efficiency of a building process. We must measure the total performance by a yardstick of total performances. We must start from the point where communications offer no limitations and when the only factors are physical ones. It is doubtful whether such conditions can be created by experiment, but they may be specified in theory. The yardstick would be an ideal, abstract one. But the comparisons made by using such an unattainable perform- ance would not be abstract, but meaningful, because they could be related to the consequences of practical experiment. These practical experiments would aim at discovering the optimum roles, con- tractual relationships, communication channels, and other conditions under which the 'ideal' is best approximated.

The nearest approach to this ideal situation would be a set of building operations managed as perfectly as possible in the interest of the client/user/community complex. Conditions would include:

(a) assembly of skills (managerial, technological and analytical), if necessary drawn from outside the industry.

(b) removal of artificial barriers in management. The designers would be part of the site management team.

(c) adequate management tools. Planning and progress data would be continuously revised and made available to all parties.

(d) abolition of conflicting interests by a structure of incentives to minimize 'defensive' action;

(e) resources for obtaining off site information;

(f) insulation from external uncertainties, for example, other projects.

(g) complete recording for later analysis of all events and actions quite separate from any management records.

Research findings resulting from the foregoing proposals will not, alone, effect changes in an industry which has, so far, not set up its own permanent research organization.

The present patterns in the industry are inherently stable. In a sense, such stability has merit for without it the industry would be subject to violent disruptions and reversals of fortune. But stable systems change too slowly for modern needs. Characteristics of the present sort of stability include the prevalent habit of crisis management—perhaps a vested interest in preserving chaos and uncertainty. It has been shown that part of this uncertainty results from actions which, in themselves, seem reasonable. An additional stabilizing factor is the set of expectations (built by experience all round) about time required, rising costs and the inevitability of conflict. Performance on any project is, therefore, unlikely to be 'better than expected' by those in charge.

It requires a massive effort to shift a system which has established a stable position at one level of performance on to a new stable position at a higher level of performance. What is needed is a demonstration that a higher standard of performance by the industry is a practicable possibility. Such a demonstration has formidable obstacles to overcome.

Research effort on a small scale may prepare the way for experiments and demonstrations on a large scale. But fragmentary efforts do not begin to measure up to the need. The proper course will be costly. How is it to be financed? The structure of the industry is not favourable to massive expenditure of the kind needed for improving overall performance, however beneficial to the community such improvement may be. This report results from the industry taking the initiative in preparatory research. But, in the final analysis, the community only gets the building industry it deserves. Therefore, the client/user/community complex also needs to associate itself with the industry in looking for the finance and providing the co-ordinating force for further large-scale research.

We consider that what we have been able to do in applying a socio-technical analysis to the building process promises useful developments. It would seem to indicate definite possibilities of identifying the more and the less effective ways of organizing work in the building team. Should these possibilities be realized, they will assist, together with operational research, in the development of models for improved relationships and communications in the industry.

But setting up models can only indicate the nature of solutions; it will not solve problems. To go further will call for a shared willingness among all the members of the building team to step forward together. Moves by one section alone cannot effect the whole change. A collaborative effort is required. The entrenched interests and institutionalized defences of all sections of the industry may suggest that collaboration is unlikely. But there are other forces at work throughout the industry which favour collaborative developments.

The Cambridge Conference, and the chain of events leading from it, support this view. We see two types of action as being required:
(a) research;
(b) collaborative leadership for change.

Research will need to be of the order envisaged by the Cambridge Conference. A mix of many disciplines and approaches would be involved. The social science/operational research combination should be part of the mix: the further development of a socio-technical analysis as a basis for building models would be a useful immediate step.

Collaborative leadership for change already has a basis in the organization set up in the name of all sections of the industry to sponsor the research already carried out. This leadership could be strengthened by efforts to mobilize those who desire change. At present, the desire for change and the willingness to collaborate have no focus. But we believe that there would be considerable response to committed leadership.

Part 4: Appendices

1. List of case studies

Site ref.	Function of building	Ongoing aspects*	Approx. contract value £000	Type of construction	Type of contract
A	Industrial	B, P, C	70	Traditional	Selective tender
B	Housing	B, P	250	Rationalized Traditional	Negotiated
G	Housing	B, P	100	Traditional	Negotiated
H	Industrial	C	500	Traditional	Selective tender
J	Education	P, C	1250	System	Selective tender
M	Health/housing	B	125	Traditional	Selective tender
N	Housing	P, C	1500	System	Negotiated
O	Housing	P, C	500	Traditional	Selective tender
P	Education	B	NA	System	Selective tender
Q	Housing	B, P, C	NA	Rationalized Traditional	All-in speculative
R	Housing	B	NA	System	Negotiated
T	Public building (extension)	B	100	Traditional	Selective tender
W	Industrial	B	NA	Traditional	Selective tender

*Ongoing aspects:
  B = brief design
  P = planning
  C = construction

NA = not available, or not applicable

2. Extracts from case studies

The case study material collected and written up during our research is so voluminous that it cannot be produced in full in this report. It must be emphasized that the material reproduced here represents only a tiny proportion of the work investigated by the research team. The thirteen projects observed, of which five were studied in great detail, are listed in Appendix 1. From these five have been selected:
(a) A housing project—brief and design stage—£¼ million: rationalized traditional construction: negotiated tender. This example is chosen to show the effects of sequential decision-taking and is related to our thesis on A I D A (Analysis of Interconnected Decision Areas) which is explained in pages 27-33 of the report.
(b) Random extracts from a number of other case studies to illustrate specific examples of communication failures referred to in the report.

A housing project—brief and design stage
This study was concerned with the design of a terraced house to be built on a large scale. The design exploration lasted eight months. The brief included:
(a) brick and timber houses;
(b) segregation of roadways and communal space (greenways);
(c) individual houses to have access to roadways and greenways;
(d) no blank walls at front or rear;
(e) minimum wet trade construction;
(f) Parker Morris standards.
   The provision of Parker Morris standards and dual access produced a quick decision to separate living and working areas with a core unit containing services. But this implied wide frontages, and the design group had information that wide frontage housing was more expensive than narrow frontage. The design group accepted the wide frontage, although this would require savings to be made by simplicity of shape and building process. A grid system was decided on and sketch designs were produced by the following sequence:

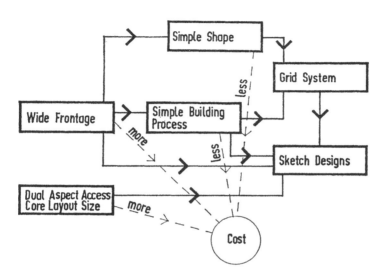

Figure 8

The group then laid down the order in which the main element of the house would be considered in more detail, as follows:

Figure 9

Lessons learnt at each stage were passed on to the next stage. Design of the individual main elements proceeded as follows:

Crosswalls: The terms of reference, sound insulation and fire regulations were factors affecting the design.

Upper floor construction: Alternatives were offered by the direction of span of the load-bearing members and by the materials, thus: direction of span could be either between crosswalls or between the external front and back walls. The materials considered were:

(*a*) Plank and beam with either 2 crosswall beams with 2" planks,
                     or   1 crosswall beam with $2\frac{1}{2}$" planks,
                     or   3 external wall beams with 3" planks.

(*b*) Board and joist with joists at 18" centres spanning crosswalls,
                     or   joists at 18" centres spanning external walls.

(*c*) Panel and joist with joists at 18" centres spanning crosswalls,
                     or   joists at 18" centres spanning external walls.

All three plank and beam alternatives were eliminated on cost grounds.

The decision to use joists involved alternatives in the choice of direction of span of load-bearing members. The crosswalls were strong enough to take the imposed weight of floor joists spanning between them, and load-bearing external walls were rejected on cost grounds.

The resulting rough layout at this stage was, therefore, as shown opposite:

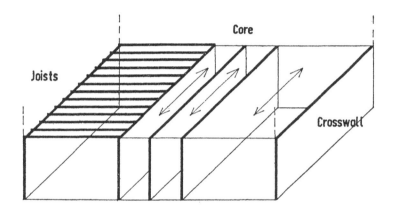

Figure 10

Roof: The alternatives for the roof were flat, monopitch, duopitch. The flat roof was rejected on cost of waterproofing and prejudice. The monopitch was quickly accepted because of the following assumed savings:

(*a*) less timber if constructed on 'inclined floor' principle;

(*b*) less drainage cost by confining stormwater to one side only of the house;

(*c*) possibility of dispensing with an internal ceiling;

(*d*) good appearance.

The first problem to arise was the high cost of materials that would withstand weather at the low pitch required to comply with (*c*). Higher pitches would cost less to weatherproof, but more to ceil, and they were usually not acceptable to the design group.

The second problem was how to support the roof. The external walls were non-load-bearing. The two possible options were, therefore:

(*a*) to take the weight on joists to the crosswalls with a load-bearing core partition on the upper floor;
(*b*) to take the weight on joists direct to crosswalls without a load-bearing upper floor partition, but this would involve counter-battens, intermediate core supports and extra cost.

The duopitch roof had been rejected on assumed cost grounds.

The problems were struggled with for a long time. The design group even considered changing decisions that had been settled, such as making the external walls load-bearing and raising the pitch and adding internal ceilings, The group then questioned the assumed savings that had led them to choose a monopitch roof. This re-investigation of a topic assumed to be settled proved to be a major step. The results showed that the cost of monopitch and duopitch were about equal. Design exploration proceeded on the lines of a duopitch.

On close study the timber content of the duopitch roof was found to be smaller with the external walls made load-bearing. So, despite previous decisions to the contrary, the external walls were made load-bearing.

External walls: The first problem was the size of the panels. The choice between two-storey or one-storey panels involved:
(*a*) size of panel that could be handled;
(*b*) support provided by panels during erection;
(*c*) part or total cladding of panels before erection;
(*d*) simplicity for manufacture.

Schedules of the numbers of variants were prepared and the group accepted one-storey panels because of the smaller range of types required, the case of precladding and the adaptation factor for single-storey housing. Core partitions and services presented no major problems and the scheme proceeded to final design stage.

Random extracts from various case studies

Interdependence within and outside the industry
The following case study extract illustrates well the effects of uncertainty and interdependence within the industry, and uncertainty
from outside.

At a first meeting of architects, quantity surveyors and contractors,
relating to the redevelopment of a site (value of scheme £150,000–
£200,000), on a negotiated basis, the programme envisaged—start
work on site autumn 1963, complete work on site autumn 1964.

The possibility that another authority might acquire part of the
site (which would have resulted in a complete change of layout)
deferred progress on the scheme until September 1963. Local
authority requirements for carparks necessitated replacement of
some houses by flats. Cost checks then necessitated changes in
typical house design: the above factor delayed starting on Bills of
Quantities by five months. The provisional start on site was delayed
by six months. Then, in the month that site work was due to start,
a Right of Way (dating from 1579 with a 392-year lease to 1971)
was discovered across the corner of the site. The owners of the land
who could reclaim in 1971 were not known.

Production of working drawings was allowed to lag during the
ensuing legal delays. The feasible starting-date was agreed as autumn
1964, one year late. But the Finance Committee's decision to reduce
the cost of one unit meant revised design and delay in programme
for this unit (a church hall). Continuing legalities in connection with
land acquisition delayed the start for a further month. Demolition
works that had been agreed were cancelled.

Late in 1964 the contractors submitted a price. The contractor,
quantity surveyor and architect changed the design, specification and
planning to save $17\frac{1}{2}\%$ of the tender figure.

Meanwhile, the architect received revised instructions about the
church hall design and, after discussion at a meeting in March 1965,
it was agreed that the views of the client's council be sought on the
advisability of proceeding with a study of alternative forms of semi-
permanent building. At this meeting (the contractors were not

invited), the quantity surveyor said that a further reduction would be achieved if the bills were sent out to tender. It was agreed that the architects and quantity surveyors should modify the scheme and that the revised bills should be sent out to tender.

As a result of competitive tender (the original contractor included), the estimate was reduced by a further 20%, of which the final modification referred to above accounted for only a small fraction.

Uncertainty from outside the building process

The initial design thinking, related to an educational project, was influenced by the desirability of architectural good manners as regards existing buildings, local traditional styles of the nearby village, and a series of large buildings of striking design on a neighbouring site.

The architects favoured a community of traditionally-built units set into the sloping site. After showing initial reluctance to the architect's ideas, the clients accepted the opportunties provided for landscaping.

The architects considered 44 months to be the most optimistic programme estimate for design and construction. But the client, having accepted the principle of traditional building, suddenly realized that educational requirements necessitated completion in 40 months—a delay of even a few months in completion would have meant a year's loss of educational facilities.

The architects suggested system building which, although no cheaper, would be quicker and easier to document.

After reluctance by the client organization to accept 'prefab' type of building, the system idea was accepted by the client's key representative, and the architects started design. The prejudice of other sections of the client organization had yet to be overcome. There followed protracted argument and discussion with various committees—principally concerning the flat roof concept. However, sketch plans were produced and submitted in time to each committee. All, except one, after further intense discussion, accepted. The one objected that prefabs would spoil the landscape, but was overruled and the project was authorized.

Two days later, an anti-system campaign was started by the local press and, following pressure by preservation groups, a public inquiry was announced. At the request of the Education Committee, the architects continued working—chiefly on those parts of the job which would be unaffected by a change of site. During the inquiry, it was found that the proposed site was in the scheduled Green Belt, and planning permission had not been obtained from the local authority. The inquiry confined itself to this aspect, rather than to the appearance of the buildings. Eventually permission to build was granted, subject to elevational approval by another independent body: this approval was granted fourteen months after the client's initial agreement to traditional building.

Eventually, a starting-date nine months ahead was called for. Then the Educational Authority called for additions which increase the size of the project by about 30% to £1¼ million.

Prior to this, tenders had been received. In the month scheduled for starting on site, a contractor was awarded the job on the basis of his tender for the smaller amount of work.

Uncertainty within the building team—drawings

(*a*) Intensive study on site revealed instances of delay and uncertainty arising from drawings. For example, on one project, at or about the time of starting on site, the contractor had received provisional sub-structure drawings and some super-structure plans from the architects. He had also the 'system' drawings. But difficulty arose in relating system drawings to architects' plans—the system drawings contained irrelevant information, e.g. many more types of windows were detailed than were required for this job: complexities of coding created difficulties in locating corresponding details on the system drawings: there was also difficulty in relating architects' super-structure elevations to structural engineers' substructure elevations. (*b*) In another study, foremen complained that the scale (8′ 0″=1″)

of drawings provided for laying drains and cable ducts was too small and caused them to work slowly to avoid mistakes.

(c) There were also complaints about structural engineering drawings, on which grid lines, wall lines, lines marking the toe of a wall and lines showing reinforcement, land drains and water bars were inadequately defined. The site copy had crease marks on it.

(d) Omission by the architect of system code numbers from a revised drawing caused delay, in another instance, in drawing up a schedule of cladding panels.

(e) Failure by the architect to send to the contractor copies of drawings sent to the suppliers of steel base plates some seven weeks previously resulted in incorrect working and failure to supply cleats and fixing bolts. This mix-up resulted in the steel erection labour leaving the site.

(f) A site foreman checking cable duct requirements noted a connection which had not been present in earlier large-scale drawings. The Clerk of Works confirmed that a drawing was still awaited from the architect, but had passed on his own copy (received that day) to the foreman. The slab was due for pouring. But, as a result of the mix-up over drawings, there was delay while extra fittings were obtained and fixed.

(g) A plumbing sub-contractor asked for more information on sanitary and waste installations, since the isometric sketches were insufficient; he was reminded by the architect that he had stated at the outset that his firm, as experts, would only require isometrics. The architect regretted that the sub-contractor's statement had not been in writing.

(h) A 3″ discrepancy in the height of a top storey on a structural drawing was found to be a draughtsman's error . . . a boiler base laid in accordance with a consulting engineer's drawing was too large . . . an electrical sub-contractor asked for drawings showing light points. The architect said they had been issued but apparently this sub-contractor had not received them.

Materials

It was noticed that a newly-delivered load of sand was a darker colour than sand that had been previously delivered. A silt test showed the sand to be unsatisfactory. The defective sand was removed, but not before part had been used in the building's substructure. It was then arranged that the store-keeper be given a sample of good sand for comparison with subsequent loads.

On one site the carpenters' shop ran out of nails. The suppliers explained that, although they were expecting delivery at their local depot from their central depot later that day, a fresh supply of nails could not be sent to the site until the following day because of the time needed to unload the delivery from the central depot, and reload onto the local lorry. The central depot lorry was not allowed to deliver to sites, even in a case such as this, where the quantity required was 5 cwt.

A contractor had ordered $4'' \times 1\frac{1}{2}''$ nominal floor boarding, but the suppliers had received a preliminary sketch from the architects which showed the floor boarding to be $4'' \times 1\frac{7}{16}''$ finished. The suppliers explained that, to achieve $1\frac{7}{16}''$ finished timber, would involve planing down from $1\frac{1}{4}''$, and that the cost would be approximately 8% more. The problem was resolved by using the timber originally ordered and the suppliers were asked to send the best finished size they could manage. As a result, time was later wasted in sorting out loads of timber, most of which measured $1\frac{7}{16}''$, but with some of $1\frac{3}{8}''$.

A contractor stated that building was being held up for lack of drainage fittings. The plumbing contractors denied this. The contractors' foreman stated that the site plumber had definitely been short of a crucial fitting. But it was found that the site foreman had not bothered to ask for one of these fittings to be brought from the sub-contractors' yard because he expected a request for the fitting to be made by the contractors' foreman.

The laying of the floor slab to the building was, as a result, held up for 10 days.

A lorry was sent to a site by the structural steel supplier to collect surplus material. A check showed that, although there were about 100 beams surplus to immediate requirements, it was not clear how many would be needed for later blocks. It was decided to send the lorry away empty and to clarify the position before the next load arrived, any surplus material being taken away at that time. The next day, despite agreement on deliveries made previously, the erectors ran out of fixing cleats. It was found that the supplier arranged his deliveries so that the sundry items, such as nuts, bolts, cotters, fixing cleats, were always on the last load of any block.

On another project the contractor contacted the supplier of metal window frames, as distinct from 'system' windows, in September. These had been scheduled for delivery in mid-August. But, as the wooden system windows had also been delayed, the non-arrival of the metal frames had not caused any worry. Now, however, the supplier of the metal frames advised the contractor that there had been difficulties and that the first delivery would be made in mid-October.

Early in October, manufactured units, which were to be fitted adjacent to the system wood windows, were found to be suitable only for the older type of windows. The manufacturer had not been informed of the changed design.

It was minuted that, despite pressure from the architect and contractor, the supplier of the system windows could still not give a firm delivery schedule. The contractor stated that the tile cladding and glazing work was being held up which, in turn, was preventing the commencement of internal partitioning. This was causing considerable standing time by the contractors' men and, since the release of scaffolding was going to be behind programme, it would be necessary for extra scaffolding to be hired.

In November, it was minuted that the system window deliveries were beginning to catch up with steel erection, but, unfortunately, isolated errors in manufacture were still causing delay. Excessive examination of the windows was being carried out by the Clerk of Works, and remedial work, such as drilling and counter-sinking and planing to allow for entry of metal windows, etc., was quite often necessary.

The metal windows varied from the issued drawings in respect of fixing screws.

In January, the contractor reported that all system windows, except for one block, had been delivered, but that workmanship was getting progressively worse with each delivery. The contractor was unable to reject the windows, owing to shortage of time, and was having to allocate valuable carpenters' time for rectifying windows on site.

A demonstration of partitioning had been arranged on one site. The demonstrators arrived late, due to a transport breakdown, only to discover that the manufacturers of the partitioning had only sent one size of panel. A further demonstration was arranged for a later date.

The contractors advised the architect that a supplier had informed him that the materials called for on the job had been taken off his standard range. The materials were now raised in price by about 10%.

A delivery of bricks was received, some of which were badly chipped. Extra work was required to sort out unusable bricks.

A window sub-contractor stated that several units were missing from site. He was to arrange for the manufacture of replacement units. He reported that the lost units were valued at nearly £600. Proof of manufacture and dispatch was available, and it must be presumed that the units were stolen in transit. Replacements were being manufactured, but would not be available for six weeks. The architect pointed out that no claim could be made against the client for the cost of replacements, nor could any extension of time be entertained for the delay caused.

Delays were experienced due to non-delivery of lino tiles. The supplies suffered faults in the curing process at their works, and tiles were being delayed by 10 days. All subsequent trades on site were affected.

A change in the specification of some kitchen equipment was noted. The architect stated that the original equipment quoted for was not now in production, and pointed out to the sub-contractor/

supplier that the tea trolleys were the wrong colour, The sub-contractor/supplier of the kitchen equipment said that he could find no reference in his records to a specific colour for the tea trolleys. He was assured by the architect that white ones had definitely been agreed, and was asked to remove the others immediately. Later, the sub-contractor/supplier of the kitchen equipment was asked by the architect why his fixers were not on the site. He stated that he had no knowledge of their whereabouts. The architect expressed dis-satisfaction with the way the kitchen equipment installation was proceeding.

3. Self-induced uncertainty in an order and supply system

The calculations described in this Appendix have been prepared in order to illustrate how uncertainties and instabilities in supply can be generated by the way in which information is communicated. It is well known, for instance, that news of an impending shortage of some material can give rise to increased orders of a precautionary nature. Such orders help to create the shortage against which they were intended to afford protection. A retailer holding stocks can interpret an increase in demand (or orders) as a signal to increase his stocks, thereby adding to the amount he is buying to meet direct orders. In these and other ways, actions which seem rational and reasonable to those who take them have the effect of generating increased demand.

These effects can be studied objectively by creating a mathematical model of the flow of goods and orders through a supply system, and by calculating how the system responds to changes in demands.

As an example, let us consider the manufacture, stocking, and sale of a hypothetical product, and the way in which this supply system responds to a change in the level of demand. We will suppose that orders are handled, and goods dispatched, according to the time lags and other characteristics depicted in *Figure 11*. Thus, delivery from the retailer is ex-stock and takes place one week from receipt of order.   Periodically, an analysis of sales is made to determine the size of order to be placed with the main distributor, so as:

(*a*) to replace the goods sold;

(*b*) to adjust stock levels in accordance with the level of business;

(*c*) to fill the 'pipeline'.

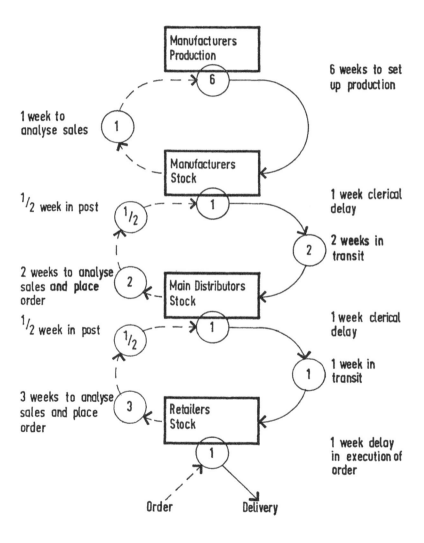

Figure 11 A supply/demand system

Thus a period of three weeks may elapse after a sale before any information (in the form of an order) reaches the main distributor. The main distributor, after assessing his stock and demand position, in turn places periodic demands on the manufacturer, who, depending on his stock position, may, after further delay, change his factory output by adjusting the rate of manufacture. *Figure 11* also shows the movement of goods from the factory to the retailer's stock, and the time these movements take. The important thing to note is that this system contains several different kinds of elements, such as goods, people, transport, and, most important, information.

Let us now see how the system responds to an increase in sales. This is depicted in *Figure 12;* the sales are shown there as having jumped by 10% in Week 10 and staying at this new, higher level. The retailer begins to respond by placing larger orders within a few weeks, but full realization that demand has increased comes later and, because stocks are being depleted in the meantime, retailer's orders to catch up with the new position reach a peak level of 18% increase by Week 23 after which they begin to settle down to the new level. The main distributor feels the effects rather later, however, and his orders reach their peak of 34% by Week 25. By the time the factory production rate has started to respond, the pipeline needs refilling and, as a result, increased production reaches a peak of 45% at Week 31, about five months after the first 10% increase in demand.

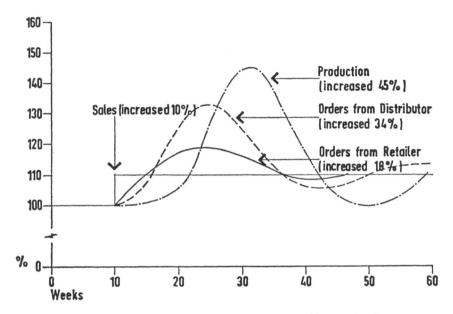

Figure 12   Response of a supply/demand system to a 10% increase in sales

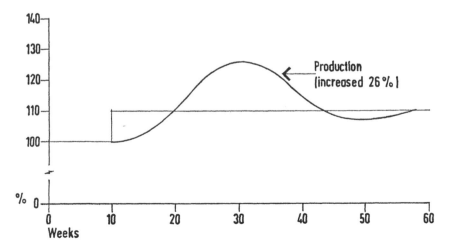

Figure 13   Effect of passing retailer's orders direct to factory

These systems behave somewhat violently and this behaviour is a consequence of the way in which the system is put together and of the demands placed upon it by the outside world. We might say that, in exhibiting such behaviour, the system is more than the sum total of its component parts. Change the flow of communications in the system and its behaviour will change. In *Figure 13*, for example, the effect is shown of passing orders direct from retailers to the factory (or of market research to achieve a similar effect). The reduced delays mean that the upswing in factory output is much less pronounced, as is the subsequent downward movement.

In real life, of course, sales show more complicated movements than in this hypothetical example, with upward and downward trends, seasonal swings, and random up and down movements. Stock control policies, too, can be of a more complicated nature. The method illustrated here can, nevertheless, provide the means for predicting the effects of changes in the flow of information in a supply/demand system and thus show the directions in which improvement should be sought.

4. Members of the Communications Research Committee

(sc denotes those members who were also members of the Steering Committee)

Chairman
The Rt. Hon. the Lord James of
Rusholme
Vice-Chancellor,
University of York

J. F. Bradford
Managing Director,
F. Bradford & Co. Ltd,
Reinforced Concrete Engineers &
Contractors

sc Eric Caswell
Chairman,
The Metal Window Association Ltd

R. Chapman
Deputy Chairman & Managing
Director,
Page Calnan & Co. Ltd,
Builders' Merchants

A. B. Cherns
Scientific Secretary,
Social Science Research Council

sc Andrew Derbyshire
(Chairman Steering Committee)
Partner,
Robert Matthew, Johnson-Marshall
& Partners,
Chartered Architects

sc J. B. Dick
Deputy Chief Scientific Officer,
Building Research Station

Basil Engert
Chairman,
Engert & Rolfe Ltd,
Roofing Felt & Asphalt
Manufacturers

Stanley Farrow OBE
Chairman,
Howard Farrow Ltd,
Civil Engineering & Building
Contractors

P. W. Grafton
Partner,
G. D. Walford & Partners,
Chartered Quantity Surveyors

The Rt. Hon. the Lord Holford of
Kemp Town ARA
Partner,
William Holford & Partners,
Chartered Architects

sc J. P. Inglis
Director,
The Drake & Scull Engineering
Co. Ltd,
Electrical, Mechanical & Sanitary
Engineers

J. W. J. Leslie
Partner,
Barlow, Leslie & Partners,
Consulting Engineers

sc Frank Newby
Partner,
Felix J. Samuely & Partners,
Consulting Engineers

sc D. E. Woodbine Parish CBE
Managing Director,
Bovis Holdings Ltd,
Building Contractors

sc E. R. Parrinder
Partner,
Davis, Belfield & Everest,
Chartered Quantity Surveyors

sc **W. J. Reiners**
Director of Research & Information,
Directorate-General of Research &
Development,
Ministry of Public Building & Works

W. H. Shouksmith
Managing Director,
J. H. Shouksmith & Sons Ltd,
Plumbers & Glaziers

R. T. Walters CBE
Deputy Director-General of Research
& Development,
Ministry of Public Building & Works

Harry Weaver
General Secretary,
National Federation of Building
Trades Operatives

Secretary
A. M. Lewis
Under-Secretary, Professional
Services Department,
Royal Institute of British Architects

Trustees of the Building Industry Communications Research Project

The Rt. Hon. the Lord Holford of Kemp Town ARA: Convener of Trustees
Sir Hugh Beaver KBE
Sir Harold Emmerson GCB, KCVO
Sir Harry Pilkington
D. E. Woodbine Parish CBE
Cyril Sweett

For Product Safety Concerns and Information please contact our EU
representative GPSR@taylorandfrancis.com Taylor & Francis Verlag GmbH,
Kaufingerstraße 24, 80331 München, Germany

Printed and bound by CPI Group (UK) Ltd, Croydon, CR0 4YY
08/05/2025
01864434-0001